The Bike Trail

Katya Calleta
Illustrated by Xiangyi Mo and Jingwen Wang

Connor and his mom had just moved to a new town.

"Do you think I'll like it here?" asked Connor. "I don't know anyone."

"I'm sure we'll both like it here," said Mom. "I have an idea. Let's go for a bike ride this morning. Let's have a picnic lunch at Lake Park."

"Okay," said Connor. "Maybe I can go swimming in the lake."

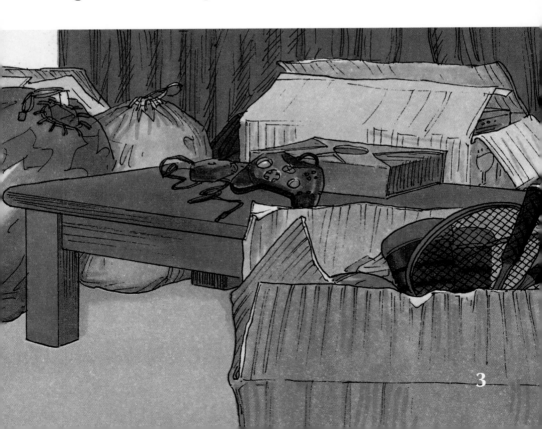

Soon Connor and his mom were
on their bikes heading west.

As they rode along, Connor looked
at the buildings in his new town.

"Look, Mom, that's my new school over there!" he said. They stopped to look at the school. Then they checked their map and rode on toward the park.

A little farther on, they came to the entrance to the park.

They stopped to look at a big map next to the entrance. It showed the lake. It also showed a lot of bike trails.

"Let's take this trail to the lake," said Mom.

"Okay," said Connor. "I can't wait to go swimming!"

Huge trees made the bike trail cool
and shady. Connor and his mom
rode along happily, enjoying the breeze.

Suddenly, as they turned a corner,
they saw a tree lying across the trail.

"The tree must have fallen down during that big storm last week," said Mom.

"It's huge!" said Connor. "It's too big to climb over or go around."

"That's for sure," said Mom.

"I really want to swim in the lake," said Connor. "Can we go back and follow another trail?"

"Okay," said Mom.

They rode back to the big map and looked at it again.

LAKE PARK
BIKE TRAILS

YOU
ARE
HERE

"We could go this way," said Connor.

He pointed at a trail on the map.

"This trail leads to the lake, too."

"Okay," said Mom. "Let's try it!"

Connor and his mom started riding again. After a few minutes, the trail began to go uphill.

They stopped to drink some water. Then they walked their bikes for a while.

"We'll be hungry by the time we get to the top of this hill," said Mom.

"That's for sure!" said Connor.

A little farther on they saw a sign.
It said, "To the Lookout."

"You know what?" said Mom.
"We might be able to see the whole
town from up there."

"I hope so!" said Connor. "And let's
have our lunch up there. I'm hungry!"

"So am I!" said Mom. "This hill is
steeper than I thought it would be."

Finally, they reached the top of the hill.
A couple of other people were having
a picnic there.

Connor and his mom went over
to look at the view.

"Wow!" said Connor. "You *can* see the whole town from up here!"

"You can see the lake, too," said Mom.

"It's beautiful up here!" said Connor.

The boy at the other picnic table came over. He was about Connor's age.

"Hi, I'm Jin," he said. "It's really nice up here, isn't it?"

"It sure is!" said Connor. "I'm Connor. My mom and I are new in town."

"Where do you live?" asked Jin.

"On Holt Street," answered Connor.

"That's not far from us," said Jin. "Look, we live on Simpson Street."

"Which school are you going to?"
asked Jin as the boys looked down
at the town.

"Central School," said Connor.

"Hey, that's my school!" said Jin.
"Look, you can see it from here."

"Maybe we'll be in the same class,"
said Connor with a big smile.

Jin's dad came over to join them. "My son and I are on our way to the lake," he said.

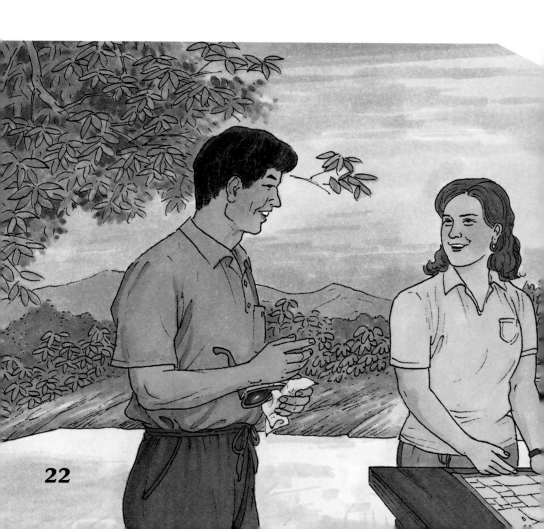

"We're going to the lake after lunch," said Connor.

"Would you like to ride to the lake with us?" Jin's dad asked. "Jin and I can show you around."

"Well, thank you. That would be great!" said Connor's mom.

"Terrific!" Connor said. "But can we eat lunch first, please? I'm hungry!"